THE CROSS HAS

THE

Final WORD

YDALIA JUAREZ ESCALERA

"Bless the Lord, O my soul; And all that is within me,
bless His holy name! Bless the Lord, O my soul, and
forget not all His benefits; Who forgives all your
iniquities; Who heals all your disease; Who redeems
your life from destruction; who crowns you with
lovingkindness and tender mercies;"

Psalm 103:1-4

Table of Contents

"My Testimony of Believing God for a Miracle"

This is my testimony of how this book came into existence.

"The Cross Has the Final Word"

On May 06, 2016, Friday morning, it was a powerful transformation. My son Elijah was so excited to recognize the Sign of the Cross next to my bed to assure me that God heard our prayers. He said, "Mom God showed himself to us, to assure you Mom that you are healed, and he intended for you to be well, and this is your testimony." The more I got to know God and how he is so phenomenal and amazing and how close God really is to us. He hears our prayers, and he knows the desires of our heart. It is a reminder for us, the Cross means a lot that "It is finished." He paid it all.

Jesus' offering was His body, prepared by God to be sacrificed on the cross. He also had to be free of infirmities in order to bear our diseases and sickness. It readily affects what He said to me "It is well with my soul." I am determined to be obedient to value God's plan.

Jesus, I will make room for you to do whatever you want me to do for your purpose according to your will. He promises me that *"I can do all things through Christ who strengthens me." (Philippians 4:13)*

I'm telling you this testimony because I wonder what's happening in your life right now. If God is moving in my life, he is moving in yours as well. He loves me, and He loves you too. I know God is always working in our lives. He moves mountains and many storms to heal us from sickness; to set the captives free. He reminds us that He is Real, and He is Alive to manifest His Glory. I was willing to be led by the Holy Spirit on how to write a book because my grammar was not too perfect.

I waited a long time to write my first book because, I understood that it takes time to develop a mature relationship with the Holy Spirit. I have dragged this process about for a long time because I felt unqualified, but I needed to be faithful and to encourage myself to do it in FAITH. I realized that it would be more sensible to wait upon the Lord until I felt sure that I could maintain a close relationship with the Holy Spirit and retain the supernatural power to be received in my life. God would gently remind me that I had a message to share the gospel around the world.

During my childhood, I learned a lot of bible stories about Jesus. I learned that He performed many miracles, healed the leper, cured two blind men, cured the paralyzed man, raised Lazarus from the dead and turned water into wine, and calmed the storm. Jesus healed each one who came to Him, and once they were healed, Jesus acknowledged their faith. I believe God will do the same thing for us to raise up, to heal our broken wounds. God will carry us through every storm and give us the strength to experience God's peace and comfort, to surround us with His love, grace, and goodness. I continually pray and ask God to give me the spirit of wisdom and knowledge; the revelation on how to name each chapter of the book.

I believe that all of these chapters have a radical message that God has ordained and placed in my heart to encourage you and to give you hope.

Chapter 1: "I Am Not Alone." God promises us he will never leave us nor forsake us.
Chapter 2: "Fight the Good Fight of Faith." I had to persevere to have faith for my health to do God's purpose.

Chapter 3: "Peace Through Pain." I have learned to be at peace in the midst of pain.

Chapter 4: "Faith of The Father's Love." My earthly father believes our Heavenly Father will heal me to perform miracles in Jesus' name.

Chapter 5: "Forgive Others." We forgive others because God forgave us.

Chapter 6: "Overcome by the Blood of the Lamb." Through the blood of Jesus, we are made whole and clean, as white as snow.

Chapter 7: "It's Finished at the Cross." God has completely wiped away our sin and sickness; he wiped our slate clean because of what Jesus did on the Cross.

Every chapter of this book will inspire you because Jesus "DID IT!" He healed my body. I hope you will be encouraged by reading this book, you will feel a greater hunger and thirst for God's word. I have a great testimony throughout my journey, I faced many trials also many curveballs. My faith had to be tested and I learned to be joyful and thankful every single day of my life. God's presence provides comfort in times of trouble, trials and sickness.

As you turn these pages they will empower you, He is sovereign over storms and uses them for His good purposes. The scripture says in (John 11:4) When Jesus heard that, He said, "This sickness is not unto death, but for the Glory of God, that the son of God may be glorified through it." Great is our Lord and mighty in power, his understanding has no limit he shows us that it doesn't matter how strong our faith is that we will still be tested. I prayed and asked God what publishing company I was to send the book to. He answered my prayer when I was crying out on Friday night in May 2019 to send me the right publisher. I remember Saturday afternoon I was working at Dress Barn in 2019, I was crying out to God to connect me with anointed women of God. To send the publisher God had anointed for the book. Thank God for the one who helped me to publish this book.

Acknowledgments

My experience in writing this book has stretched me to grow in faith and strengthened me to wait and expect his promise. The truth is though it is only through the Grace of God that I have been kept alive to be with my husband, and my four beautiful children, also to my wonderful dad and friends that he placed in my life to help this book to become a reality.

I also encourage you to stay focused on the word of God, and believe that whatever you ask in prayer according to the will of God it will come to pass, despite what you see, hear, or feel; knowing by faith God will always keep his promise and never fail us.

(1 Corinthians 2:9) But as it is written;
"Eye has not seen, nor ear heard, nor have entered into the heart of man the things which God has prepared for those who love Him."

This scripture excites me to the greatest the promise of his love Jesus Christ, it is our hope strength, courage, and assurance that is for eternity. Now we have to receive, not the spirit of the world, but the spirit which is of God; that we might know things that are freely given to us. I had to listen to hear and to know his voice to receive the spirit of understanding by reading the word of God to grow in the principal of healing and resurrection power to overflow in my life. God says that His Word will not return void. This scripture inspires me to the fullest: ***Ephesians 3:20 "Now to him who is able to do exceedingly abundantly above all that we ask or think, according to the power that works for us."*** He knows we should stay focused on the word of God. God always brings the right people across our paths at the appropriate time and season. So many friends helped me and to whom I owe my appreciation and gratitude. I want to thank Kelvin & Barbara Elliott also Debby Jackson for their dedication and support of this book.

I want to extend my warmest thanks to all of The Stephen Ministry Team, as well as Kids Life Ministry. I'm so grateful to my dear friends from Lakewood Church who gathered beside me and my family to embrace their love, to be the hands and feet of Jesus and a true reflection of God's Love. Through the dedication of their time, they came to the hospital to visit me. Thank you for being supportive friends in my life.

I dearly appreciate and want to thank Joseph & Herlinda Martinez because they were there so faithful and committed to fasting for 21 days to believe God; for a breakthrough to declare a miracle for the condition of my health. I'm grateful to my son-in-law Adrian Luna for all the time and support during this remarkable journey of my healing.

I want to thank Liliana I. Zepeda who was in JROTC from Channelview High School and brought the students to clean up my house and her beautiful mom. I honor Pastor Lisa Osteen Comes also, Pastor Dodie Osteen for being such a great example of living a life of faith and continually praying for me and for many others that need restoration healing. How much I love you, all of you for inspiring me and for sharing your faith with me. You have been there for me and my family still standing together strong by showing me how great is our God and how he always listens to each one of us. I say thank you from the bottom of my heart for your support and together we are accomplishing great things for the Kingdom of God. Here is a scripture, I want to dedicate to each one of you, in the book of *Matthew 25: 35-36 "For I was hungry and you gave me something to eat, I was thirsty and you gave me something to drink, I was a stranger and you invited me in. I needed clothes and you clothed me, I was sick and you looked after me."*

The most important in my life is our Heavenly Father, thank you for the gifts and your compassion towards me. Thank you so much I could remember he has always been faithful to me; even when with my own eyes, I could not see; but he was always there to visit me day and night at the hospital at all times watching over me. I will not be shaken, for He is right beside me. My body rests in safety. The wonderful thing is He promised me; he will turn my joy and my tears into laughter. He will wipe away every tear from my eyes. *"You keep track of all my sorrows. You have collected all My tears in your bottle. You have recorded each one in your book." (Psalm 56:8)* I will never forget the things that he has done for me; and I will never lose my hope, and I will always hold and believe and walk in my divine health, just as my soul prospers. My greatest desire is one day I will see Jesus and I cannot wait to see Jesus to acknowledge him with a BIG Hug, and to say thank you.

Dedication

To my loving parents Benito and Audelia Juarez how much I appreciate their encouraging words. My parents never stopped praying for their fourteen children. My parents raised us with so much love and affection and they provided the best they could. I love you so much and miss you both. My Father was a great hero he defended and protected our country. He served in the United States Air Force. He would always encourage my children and for me to put God first in everything, also to be kind and to respect others. He always said, "No more war just peace. Love, no war." I enjoyed praying with my dad every morning and every night before going to bed. For four years, I dedicated myself to taking care of my dad and learned a lot from my daddy as I was his caregiver. My husband and I and my children had a lot of patience and joy during the time we cared for my daddy.

To my mother, I am so grateful and thankful to God, my mom was the first spiritual leader in our family and to build a strong foundation of faith at home and guided me to attend church. My mom always had a very caring heart and was understanding towards her children. She was a strong prayer warrior and taught me to forgive others, so God will forgive my trespasses.

Julian, my husband, and faithful friend, also the father of my four incredible blessings, my children. He helped me to be a better mother. We walked down the broken road together committed to each other despite the difficulties. You are truly the love of my life. I am blessed to be your wife!

To Magaly Michelle, Julian III, Marsha Victoria, and Elijah Joseph you are truly a big miracle, God created you to become the people he wanted you to be. I love watching you all grow into the precious people you were made to be by God. You are my daily dose of joy. I will always love you with all of my heart and to my Lord and Savior Jesus Christ, All I can say is THANK YOU!

To the memory of my loving Father-in-Law Julian V. Escalera. He was an intelligent man; an amazing provider for his family, a caring heart for his children and stood by his beautiful wife for 50 years of marriage. But God only knows how much we miss you, and we love you so much. We know you are watching over us. To my loving Mother-in-Law Juanita Escalera, how much I appreciate you, all the ways you help our family. How blessed and fortunate we are to still have you here with us to build and plant seeds of encouraging words. The beautiful heart you have for your grandchildren and great-grandchildren; I will always appreciate you and love you so much.

To Meme Spearman for her dedication to this vision and for believing in me. I'm grateful that God brought us together and connected us through this project to present God's message; to share my testimony; to encourage others and to bring hope, love and compassion to our world.

I constantly had to speak the word of God into myself to believe for miraculous healing. Every breath I take I will give thanks to God above for as long as I shall live, I will testify to his love and encourage myself regarding how God made a way for me to testify. I know that I know, God healed me from the top of my head to the soles of my feet. He can heal you too. God used me to pray for a patient next to my bed at the hospital, she said can you pray for me because she had heavy pains in her stomach feeling the same symptoms I had. I told her just believe in your miracle let's pray and have faith. Jesus, you said, "I lay hands on the sick, and they will recover." Mark 6:5 tells us," Now He could do no mighty work there, except that he laid His hands on a few sick people and healed them." When you believe God's word and understand the calling on your life God can use you too. Also, I encourage you to stay focused on God's promises and to believe that whatever you and I ask in prayer; according to the will of God it will come to pass. Despite what I see, hear, or feel. I chose to know that God wants us to trust him, not to doubt.

God's wants for us to be well through him to receive the supernatural and his willingness to intercede for our lives. Jesus reminded me how very important it is for me to reiterate my authority to overcome Satan and sickness. It gives God's Word first place in my heart because it is life and health to my body and nourishment to my bones. Joshua 21:45, God's word will not fail. Not a word failed of any good thing which the Lord had spoken to the house of Israel. All came to pass. Early morning in my prayer time, I would wake up to meditate it was so important for me to read healing scriptures in my bible. I didn't want the word of God to depart from my mouth, always keeping it inside my heart, because it helped me to breathe life into my health. The bible says in Deuteronomy 7:15 "The Lord will remove from you all sickness and he will not put on you any of the harmful diseases from Egypt which you have known, but he will lay them on all who hate you." You can have abundant life if you want to, but you need to know that it is God's will for you to be healed. You must establish in your mind and heart that it is God's will for you to be well. God does not play favorites. It is His will and desire for you to be healed. God has done His part to heal us. Our immediate physical healing has been bought and paid for in the death of Christ. Now it's up to us to receive that healing through faith. As I read this scripture in the book of Matthew 8:2-3 "And behold, a leper came and worshiped Him, saying, "Lord, if you are willing. You can make me clean." Then Jesus put out His hand and touched him, saying "I am willing; be cleansed." Immediately his leprosy was cleansed. It is God's will for you to be well. If you do not believe that you need to change your thinking. If you do not know the Word of God, you need to learn it; this is your time to embrace God's word. "O God, our Father, your word says that you are a very present help in time of need. I come to you now on behalf of someone who is sick, suffering, or in pain with a tumor or some another serious disease. Father, I ask you in the Name of Jesus Christ to touch them and heal. Thank you, Jesus, for healing me, because I know He loves me; I am His child. He will heal you because He loves you too. I would meditate day and night on this scripture Psalms 118: 17 "I shall not die, but live, and declare the works of the Lord." I had to encourage myself through the storms and struggles that I faced in my life. Today I can stand here firm and unwavering in faith and tell you that I still believe in miracles. Miracles happen all around us and come in many different ways. Miracles remind us of the power of God and help us to grow in faith and is a constant reminder that Jesus is always with us; even though it may be hard to believe. But he is always there for us. Some nights I remember looking out of my bedroom window. Jesus, I know you hear my cry and my petitions. Through my experiences, I have seen the hand of God working wonders and miracles on my journey. Proverbs 3:5-6 "Trust in the Lord with all your heart and lean not to your own understanding; in all your ways acknowledge Him, and He shall direct your paths."

Chapter One:
"I AM NOT ALONE"

I want to emphasize how we are not alone; Jesus is always on our side, He is waiting for us to call upon him for deliverance from sin and sickness. Jesus didn't intend for us to be alone in this dark world but, he desires that we seek him daily and have confidence in ourselves to depend on him to trust also to believe. When we are facing challenges through health conditions, the book of Ephesians says not to lose heart. I remember when I was admitted to East Houston Hospital, Jesus gave me a scripture in the Book of Isaiah 43- 1:2 "But now, thus says the Lord, who created you, and he who formed you, "Fear not, for I have redeemed you; I have called you by your name; You are Mine. When you pass through the waters, I will be with you; And through the rivers, they shall not overflow you. When you walk through the fire, you shall not be burned..." I believe with all my heart that Jesus will help us to overcome any obstacle in life until the end. At my lowest point, I felt alone, and the loneliness was overwhelming. Sometimes I would hear voices that would say to me "You are alone, and no one understands you or cares enough to visit you." I started praying Jesus, I come boldly unto the throne you said no evil can harm me, you gave me the authority to rebuke every lie of the enemy. The bible says in Romans 8:31 "What then shall we say to these things? If God is for us, who can be against us?" I didn't want to feel concerned and to be away from my family while I was at the hospital. I wanted to have a peace of mind and also confidence that I would be coming back home very soon. As, I continued praying that one of my children would come to stay with me at the hospital because I didn't want to feel alone. My oldest daughter Magaly decided to stay most of the time and my three children stayed home to support my daddy also my husband and take care of the responsibilities at home.

Magaly was in 12th grade attending Channelview High School. When she stayed most of the time with me, I told her let's pray and ask God for favor at school. For you to graduate from high school and also to open doors for scholarships and to give mommy the strength to endure this health challenge and for a big miracle. Jesus, I believe you will allow me to see my daughter Magaly graduate from high school and attend college. I prayed that God would send me close friends from Lakewood church to stand with me in agreement in prayer for my health. As I constantly read my bible John 16:32 "yet I am not alone." And yet I am not alone, because the father is with me. I am so thankful for the nurses who were there to lift me up to encourage me to stay steadfast and to know that I will be alright and not to lose my faith; knowing myself, Jesus is always there during sickness. I realized that I am not alone because God will always be with me. He reminded me of the story of Moses; when Jesus told Moses in the Book of Joshua 1:5, "No man shall be able to stand before you all the days of your life; as I was with Moses, so I will be with you. I will not leave You nor forsake you." This scripture gave me hope that wherever I go Jesus would always be beside me in the hospital bed to comfort and strengthen me and also with my family.

On Friday morning the doctors came into my room and said to me, "Mrs. Escalera you will need to stay longer, you need a procedure done. This procedure is called a "Central Line" on your right side in your arteries. You will need intravenous fluid and more testing to examine your colon. I asked the doctors, what do you mean? What is wrong with my colon please explain this to me. The doctors said, "Well, your colon is inflamed on the right side of your large intestine." I asked the doctors, during the procedure will I be awake or asleep? The doctors responded to me, "Yes; "You will be awake." I said, "Oh, No, doctor, I refuse this procedure; I don't have peace." The doctors told me, "But! Mrs.Escalera we have done this particular procedure to other patients before. I said, "I am not like those patients. Not for me. I heard the Holy Spirit speaking inside of me; You are made for more." I know it is not easy, especially when the enemy gives you lying symptoms in the area of your physical health to get you worried. Jesus promises when we choose to let go of our worries to Him and to trust him with all your heart you will see some challenges. His grace, His healing. The Lord's hands are so much bigger than ours. His grace towards us never stops flowing. I do not want to miss out, but I want to see His supply flow in every area of my life.

Friday afternoon my friend Roseana Bueno called me to let me know she was coming to visit me; I was so excited that she was coming over to the hospital. As they were driving, her husband Angel Bueno heard the Holy Spirit say; Hear this Ydalia, it will encourage you to let you know and to remind me; "I Am Not Alone." I started crying I felt the presence of God so deep inside of me and his peace. Jesus gave me the scripture in the book of 1 Corinthians 2:9 "But as it is written: Eye has not seen, nor ear heard, Nor have entered into the heart of man the things which God has prepared for those who love Him." I started to search on YouTube for the song "I AM NOT ALONE" by Kari Jobe. This song inspired me and gave me hope to know that I am not alone, he will go before me. We know that we do not fight alone, for God is He who fights for us, just as he promised us. Thank you, Jesus, that you hold the victory over sin and death in this world.

I told my husband that I was going to discharge myself out of the hospital. I said to my husband let me speak to the head nurse. I asked the head nurse, I need to know just one thing I need to know if I'm bleeding internally, and the head nurse said NO. So that is when I decided to discharge myself out of the hospital. I will follow up with the primary doctor for recommendations to a specialist to inform me of the condition of my health.

The doctors from the East Houston Hospital were not communicating with each other considering my health. I had to have peace to know for myself this was the right decision that I was making and to follow the Holy Spirit to discharge myself from the hospital. I had to know that "I Am Not Alone." I have hope and peace in my heart for this present time in my life and days yet to come. How blessed we are to know God's word is the best way to find the true answer to have confidence. I have faith in your word today and forever. Despite every discouraging symptom, my heart knew that God's word could not lie. I had confidence in God's word that says by the stripes of Jesus I am healed. I will line up with God's Word that says whatever I ask, I receive it because I keep His commandments. To find the promise of God is to read the Word of God then ask according to His will; he will hear and answer your prayer. The Word of God is so important when you are fighting a battle for your health to give you hope. You will always need the Word of God to keep you from harm, to keep you safe, to show you how to live an abundant life, and to keep you during a tragedy. I thank God that my daughter Magaly. She has been grounded in the Word of God and it is first place in her heart, and she would read the word to me for me to receive my healing. Magaly read, Romans 8:11, The Spirit of Life is making your body alive, mommy. Also, mom, Jesus answered in John 14:6, "I am the way and the truth and life. No one comes to the Father except through me." Every day you should speak the Word, pray the Word. The Word of God is the two-edged sword that is your weapon of offense with which you can defend yourself. My assurance through this time of illness was I had to know that Jesus is truly faithful. He will always be beside us and we don't have to experience fear because we are not alone. When our life is like a roller coaster do not feel discouraged. When there are hard times, affliction or challenges in life remember you are not going through this alone. No matter how you feel, if you are desperate or alone in the midst of the storm; Jesus is always right there with you. Hebrews 10:23 says, "Let us hold fast the confession of our hope without wavering, for He who promised is faithful."

If you do not know the Word of God or know that it is God's will for you to be healed; if you will live in vital union with Him, He will help you overcome all of your problems and to live in victory. As I walk in union with God and His purpose for my life, I know He will nourish and sustain me in every situation and circumstance. In those days when Hezekiah became ill and was at the point of death; in 2 Kings 20:6, God reveals to us that Hezekiah was not alone because the prophet Isaiah the son of Amoz came to him, and said unto him, "This is what the Lord says: Set your house in order, because you are going to die; you will not recover." 2) Hezekiah turned his face to the wall and prayed to the Lord, saying 3) remember now how I have walked before you faithfully and with a perfect heart, and have done what is good in your eyes. And Hezekiah wept. 4) And it came to pass after Isaiah was gone out into the middle court, that the word of the Lord came to him, saying 5) Go back and tell Hezekiah, the captain of my people, this is what the Lord, the God of your father David, I have heard the prayer, I have seen your tears; I will heal you. On the third day from now, you will go up to the temple of the Lord. 6) And I will add fifteen years to your life. And I will deliver you and this city from the hand of the king of Assyria; and I will defend this city for mine own sake, and my servant David's sake. And Isaiah said unto Hezekiah, Hear the word of the Lord."

He loves you so much, he will not forget about you. It is for us to realize how valuable we are to God; therefore, he will not leave us alone. As I experience a relationship with God I am fulfilled in my heart and receiving all I need for my health. I need to seek him daily in my personal experiences and His love for me. We just need to follow Christ and be devoted to building our body, with one mind, one spirit, one purpose, and one goal; to know God. We will know the Son of God as we build on the foundation of freedom. Jesus is so wonderful and mighty to allow his endurance to fulfill our lives with joy and our hearts to receive his love. When we are in the wilderness in a desert land; Jesus cared for us and guarded us as the pupils of His eyes. Psalm 32:7, "You are my hiding place; you preserve me from trouble; you surround me with songs of deliverance." This song "Milagroso abres Camino" in English it means "Way Maker" it changed my emotion, knowing Jesus is moving in our midst is the answer to it all. How God is divine to my purpose, a way maker, my miracle, my testimony. How God set me free from Colitis and for me to know that "I Am Not Alone" through the midst of the storm.

I choose to live my life to enlighten others about my healing; to receive the Power of the Holy Spirit; to know the joy inside of me. When I let my light shine before men, God can perform wonderful miracles in my life as well as others. Your light attracts others to you because God, who is Light, dwells in you, and your light will never go out. In the Book of Matthew 5:14, "You are the light of the world. A city that is set on a hill cannot be hidden. Let your light so shine before men, that they may see your good works and glorify your Father in heaven." Your words are light and life to me, O' God, my Healer, and my Salvation. How I praise You for restoring and giving me hope, and for the recovery of my health and my life and to enlighten others: to share hope and to help others. Thank you, Jesus, for "I Am Not Alone" in my life and for miraculously transforming me and surrounding me with your love. And I hope that this chapter will be a means of bringing hope to your heart, and always know that Jesus will never change.

Chapter Two:
"FIGHT THE GOOD FIGHT OF FAITH"

I was battling with a sickness in my stomach not knowing what caused the pain. I continued carrying out a normal life. I attended Lakewood Church for almost 24 years. Through the time of the illness, I continually served in Stephen's Ministry. I thank God for giving me the strength and the ability to pray for others and serve faithfully. There were some Sunday services, I could not serve others because I was not in the best condition to pray, I was feeling so much pain on the right side of my stomach. I would go to the prayer line with Pastor Steve and Suzie Austin to agree with me for a supernatural healing. I shall live by faith Your word is life to me and health to my flesh. Jesus, I believe in you, that you would heal me of every disease and make me whole again, because I couldn't eat anything. I was in so much pain and taking medications that were not helping the pain go away. I would pray and say to God, you created me you've known me since the foundation in my mother's womb. Jesus, you know that I am a Mexican and I was raised with rice, beans and flour tortillas. I said, "Jesus, I'm asking you in faith to restore my appetite to eat again because I love to eat."

So, on Sunday morning, December 6, 2015, I got a scripture on my phone, and it was the book of Hosea 4:6, and the Lord spoke to me and said, "Your faith is strong, but my people are destroyed because of lack of knowledge." After reading this, I told my husband "You know honey we need to go to the hospital because I'm not feeling well. I'm in so much pain." When I got to the hospital, I was hoping it would be something minor, like an infection in my stomach and to be discharged from the hospital that same day. I didn't want to stay longer at the hospital. But Jesus knew that I needed to have faith in him to persevere through the pain and not to lose my faith. I remember calling Lisa Salazar to agree with me in prayer because I was in serious pain. So, the doctors decided to do an ultrasound of my stomach, and when the results came back the nurses and doctors told me that I had colitis and inflammation in my colon. They told me that I had to be admitted to the hospital and I told the doctors, "Oh, oh no Jesus, I don't have time for this, I'm planning to celebrate my daughter Marsha's "Quinceanera." But against all my emotions, I remained at the hospital as nurses were monitoring my condition. Three days later, I decided to discharge myself from the hospital because it was my daughter Marsha's time to celebrate her Quinceanera on December 18, 2015. I would like to thank Pastor John Gray for performing my daughter's ceremony and for speaking a word of encouragement to my daughter. I was sent home with four different kinds of medications. On January 16, 2016, I went back to the hospital because I could not stand the pain again. I called Pastor Lisa Comes and asked for her to please stand in agreement in prayer with me for a supernatural healing in my body. I felt the same pain in my stomach again, so I was admitted back again into the hospital. Doctors requested to perform a procedure, an ultrasound to identify and obtain images of the structures causing the pain inside my stomach. So, I was diagnosed again with Colitis, a small tumor.

On Thursday night, God reminded me that "I Am Not Forgotten." I started to hear the Holy Spirit, so I got my cell phone turned on YouTube to listen to the song by Israel Houghton. God knows what I am going through, and he is watching over me. I was praying and said, "Jesus, I believe in you, I know you have a purpose through this test but give me the grace to stand in faith." So, Friday morning I woke up and put my makeup on and was getting ready for ER Doctors and the results. As I was waiting, the doctors came into my room and gave me the results. The doctors said, "Mrs. Escalera is your husband coming this morning to visit you. I said, "No, because he is working." Well, the doctors said, "Mrs. Escalera the reason you are having so much pain in your colon is because it seems to be cancer." The doctors first diagnosis was that I had a tumor and Colitis in my colon. I told the doctors "Oh, No Doctor, I don't receive it." I said to him, "Jesus is my Alpha and Omega and knows the beginning to the end of my life." I wasn't frightened and I didn't cry because I knew it was a lie from the enemy. I remember when I was going through a very tough time four years ago and it looked like I was surely going under. I could not see in the natural any way for me to come out on top, fear was attempting to convince me that I was finished. But I decided to get alone with God and took a long walk and began to tell the Lord that I needed a word from Him because fear was knocking at the door of my mind.

This is how Jesus tells us to overcome fear by increasing our faith. Joshua 1:9, "Have I not commanded you, Be strong and courageous. Do not be afraid do not be discouraged for the Lord your God will be with you wherever we go." God actually commands us not to fear or worry. Most likely because He knows the enemy uses fear to decrease our faith, our hope and victories by limiting God. Again, my oldest daughter Magaly decided to stay with me at the hospital for a weekend, we both were praying and declaring for an 85-year-old patient next to my bed; believing for her to be healed. She was sick of a heart condition and had just gotten out of the ICU. My heart just broke down because she didn't have any family member beside her, so I started praying for family members to come and visit her. Sure enough, the family showed up early Monday morning. When the nurse's assistant checked my vitals as the nurse finished, I asked the family members if it was okay for me to pray for your mommy. They said, "Yes. Sure, please do so we believe in prayer." I asked was it okay to read you a scripture, Mark 11:24, "Therefore I tell you, whatever you ask in prayer, believe that you have received it, and it will be yours. So today we will have confidence when we pray, Jesus will hear our petitions and heal your mom." When we prayed it was so beautiful the HOLY SPIRIT showed up in the room; we got to see the light coming into the room. It was so incredible because we could feel the presence of God even the family members and the patient were feeling so much more at peace.

On that Tuesday morning, at 5:45 am she was screaming for help and asking me for assistance, so I reached out to her. She said to me, "Please pray for me again. I'm not feeling well." I started massaging her legs and started praying for her: "Jesus we come boldly unto the throne of grace asking you in faith for your daughter to be healed and restore her heart and give peace through the midst of her health so that we may obtain mercy." When we finished praying, she felt much more calm. What was so amazing on that Tuesday morning the doctors told her that she will be discharged from the hospital. I was so excited for her and thanking God for her miracle and breakthrough. Jesus promised, I can call Him in times of need. Thank You, Lord, that I can trust you to be there for me and the patient next to my bed. Later that night I prayed for myself and asked God to obtain grace to help me to get out quickly of the hospital and to be with my family and to give me the peace of God, which surpasses all my understanding and not to be anxious and to abide in faith. I have confidence in your word, and I take hold of your promises to heal me. Your Word says that Jesus bore all my sickness and disease, and he carried my sorrow, so I receive healing now; and knowing by faith declaring that Jesus is my Healer and my Deliverer.

This is my prayer, I give you all the Praise and Glory and Honor to you all days of my life to come, and to sustain me as I walk in faith, when many fiery tests and trials come. You will keep me strong. Father, I'm thankful that you are no respecter of persons. What you do for one, you will do for me. Jesus is telling us to believe and have faith the size of a mustard seed that you can speak to this mountain, to be moved from any addiction or health issues. Despite the fact that the doctors diagnosed me with colitis, I have the power to fight the good fight of faith to overcome and to stand firmly; to hold on, to be anchored with the word of God and to believe Jesus finished a good work in my health. As I pray, your word says by faith, give me the patience and confident expectation to be free from every sickness, disease, and illness. Jesus sent the Holy Spirit precisely so that we should have power to fight the good fight of faith. So, if you are experiencing a struggle along the path to your personal victory — if you've been fighting heart conditions, or diabetes, and cancer or depression along the way — don't be taken off guard or by surprise. God's will for your life is for you to give your very best effort and do whatever is necessary to receive your miracle that is set before you! I didn't know how many storms the enemy had sent to try to keep me from God and from getting to my promise and how many times God has said, "Peace be still" that is my daughter. I'm going to break those tumors also fear and break every chain, in Jesus Name. I'm going to fulfill my destiny. God has been fighting for me my whole life pushing back the forces of darkness and crossing lakes, calming storms just to get me through some of these battles that took place when I was a little girl. The enemy knew way back when that I have a calling on my life to do great things for Jesus, he could see the favor and the anointing on my life. He could see I was destined for greater, so he has worked overtime trying to stop my destiny. But I had to remember — the greater reward usually requires a greater fight.

Romans 8:28 "And we know that God causes everything to work together for the good of those who love God and are called according to his purpose for them." I keep this in mind as I press forward to the promise in my determination to overcome every obstacle and resistance along the way. I stayed in the fight until I could shout loud, "The fight is finished, and victory obtained!" You should stay in the fight until your assignment is fulfilled and you have received a miracle. I had a "good fight" the one I win, one that I'm victorious in. But the Word of God encourages us to stand strong in faith, knowing that He is backing us all the way, and the faith that He has placed within us is a victory waiting to happen. That's why the Word of God calls it a good fight - because we were destined, as children of God, to WIN. I guess you could say the fight has been fixed or rigged on our behalf. So, you can see how ridiculous it would be for us to quit, and how ridiculous it is for us NOT to have the joy of the Lord radiating throughout our lives. Victory is ours and it's just a matter of time. Father, I admit that I'm in a fight. I need grace and strength to stay in this match and finish it to completion. I didn't realize how much would be required of me. But I am determined and committed to keeping up the good fight of faith until I can say the fight is finished and victory is accomplished. "Holy Spirit, I ask You to fill me with a fresh supply of your power and anointing, strength, and resolve—a supernatural level of commitment—so I will stay in the fight until my assignment is fulfilled. The life you now live in the body in which you live, by faith in God who loves you and gave himself up for you; walk by faith and not by sight. I boldly declare that God knows exactly what I am facing. I am not fighting this good fight of faith by myself. The Holy spirit lives in me and fills me with enough power to resist any opponent that would try to stop me from fulfilling God's plan." Always delight in the Holy Spirit to fill you with a free gift of God's faith to endure strong to the end; so you and I can stay in this fight, the good fight of faith until it is over so we will win the victory.

Chapter Three:
"PEACE THROUGH PAIN"

"Words of praise are on my lips. May peace be unto me, for the Lord will heal me." Isaiah 57:19. It does not matter what the problem is, trust and pray knowing that God is in control. I had to put my trust in God on March 8, 2016. I was scheduled as an out-patient for a colonoscopy. The doctor explained to me during the exam used to detect abnormalities in the large intestine, in my colon and rectum and using a video camera to view the inside of the entire colon. During the procedure, I had to have peace in my heart and my mind and not allow any negative words or thoughts to come into my spirit. While I was in the recovery room to relax, I opened my bible to Mark 5:34 And He said to Me, "My daughter, your faith has made you well. Go in peace and be healed of your affliction." It allowed me constantly every day and every night to totally trust in God with adoration of worship and to enter into his presence with thanksgiving and praise.

During this time of desperation, I drew closer to God, and he grew closer to my side, hearing my cry. God made it clear that he was reaching out and saying to us to stand fast; his love endures forever. When we praise God before we see change, we are saying with our actions that we believe. Jesus looked at them and said, "With men this is impossible, but with God all things are possible." Matthew 19:26. I had to enter into His rest; and be seated and wait. I would remind myself, "God's got this." As I praise and magnify the name of the Lord, I'm declaring and believing that the victory is mine as I simply wait for it to manifest. To receive the evidence, I had to believe in myself and that the battle belongs to the Lord. Wednesday morning, I put on the shoes of peace, which brings healing to my body and my soul. I prayed for a trusting spirit as I did a spiritual battle over this illness. I rebuked both worry and irritation and instead decided to carry peace on the inside of me. The battle is the Lord's, so go in peace against the conditions of your health. Jesus goes with us. We invite him to fight our battles for us. We have the assurance he has given us to have the confidence to walk in peace to overcome the wiles of the devil. Knowing in faith that Jesus' healing power is coming towards us to restore our health, in Jesus' name. I declared peace into my thoughts and over my body. I spoke peace into my cells and my colon, my organs and my hormones so that my body would function well. I thank God for your peace. Jesus is able to calm the waves and cure my body, in Jesus Name. The Bible tells us in Ephesians 6:10-13, "Put on the full armor of God, so that you and I can take our stand against the wiles of the devil. Wherefore take unto you the whole armour of God, that you may be able to withstand in the evil day, and having done all, to stand your ground, and after you have done everything to stand firm."

The Helmet of Salvation will keep me from being double-minded. I put on the mind of Christ Jesus that I may be conformed to His image. **The Breastplate of Righteousness** "He made Him who knew no sin to be sin on our behalf, so that we might become the righteousness of God in Him." (2 Corinthians 5:21) **The Belt Girded with Truth** "Buy the truth and sell it not; also wisdom, and instruction and understanding." (Proverbs 23:23) **The Shoes of the Gospel** of peace is to live with confidence that we will overcome at any moment and do not let anything become slack in your walk. **The Shield of Faith** "And how shall they preach, except they be sent? as it is written, How beautiful are the feet of them that preach the gospel of peace, and bring glad tidings of good things" (Romans 10:15) **The Sword of the Spirit** "For the word of God is quick, and powerful, and sharper than any two-edged sword, discerning to the division of soul and of spirit, and of the joints and marrow." (Hebrews 5:12) Every morning as I prepared for the day, I need to dress in the Armor of God before going to the doctor's office that I will stand by faith. For I know the battle is not mine, it belongs to God. I had to choose to direct my thoughts towards your goodness and grace. I will seek God in prayer to continue to give me an extra measure of grace so that peace would flood my spirit. I need your grace to manifest in multiple ways throughout my days; to remind me of your presence and peace; to reflect your image in Christ. What God wants you and me to do is to take our position and no matter how things are or what we are facing; the giants, to maintain that position of peace. I will lift my hands to surrender all that I have to praise you to give you all my heart and my soul to live for you alone. In the midnight hour, I will worship you in my house, I will worship him everywhere I am; because every breath that I take it comes from you, every moment that I am awake, I will praise you. God, I know you are in control over my pain and sickness to dry up all cancer cells.

On March 8, 2016, I had an appointment with a Gastroenterologist to inform me of the results. The doctor said, "Mrs. Escalera the reason you are having so much pain in your stomach is because there is a tumor the size of a golf ball, you need to have surgery to remove it. Mrs. Escalera do you have any questions for me?" No! But it's okay doctor, I know God will help me as I go through this because he knows from the beginning to the end of my life. The Doctor referred me to a Surgeon to schedule me for surgery. Jesus reminded me of this scripture, in the book of 1 John 5:14-15 "If we ask anything according to his will, he hears us..." Whatever we ask in faith we know that we shall have it when we ask in Jesus' name. I told my husband we need to pray to direct us to the right doctors for the surgery. As I was leaving the doctor's office walking towards the elevators with my husband and my oldest daughter Magaly. I heard the Holy Spirit say, "Put everything in God's hands the worries and sickness also the Doctors and know God's in control over everything." My husband and I also my daughter got into our car KSBJ was playing the song "Joy of the Lord" by

Rend Collective. The meaning of the song is found in the book of Nehemiah 8:10, "The joy of the Lord is my strength" It helped me to understand the book of Nehemiah to experience the joy of the Lord no matter if the physical evidence is there to rely on it will only come from an inner strength provided by the Lord. Jesus experienced the fulfilling joy that stemmed from His Father's strength and wanted us to be filled and overflowing with it. John 15:11

Psalm 56:4

"In God I will praise his word
In God I have put my trust, I will not fear
What flesh can do unto me."

I am delivered from all of my fears, and I'm surrounded with the peace of freedom. Jesus split the sea so I could walk through it; I receive the peace of his perfect love. "Humble yourselves, therefore, under God's mighty hand, that he may lift you up in due time. Cast all your anxiety on him because he cares for you." 1 Peter 5:6-7, Jesus is so precious to me. When I opened my bible Jesus gave me a scripture in the book of Isaiah 41:10, "Fear not, for I am with you; Be not dismayed, for I am your God. I will strengthen you, yes, I will help you, I will uphold you with My righteous right hand." When we pray to God before we hear negative reports from the doctor, we are to speak life with our mouths. Words of gratitude; thank you Jesus that he has a perfect plan for us, and it is better than anything that we could plan for ourselves, because he is still performing wonder working miracles. I choose to walk in the peace and freedom of your spirit and not be overcome with fear and anxious thoughts. I will take your shield of faith so that I can extinguish all the darts and threats coming my way by the enemy. Jesus remains the same yesterday, today, and forever; he is the everlasting God. No matter what we face in life or what is going on around us we do not need to be afraid. We may not like it, but we can handle it because Jesus can handle it and He gives us full access to His peace. As Jesus said, "These things I have spoken to you so that in me you may have peace. Peace, I leave with you; My peace I give to you not as the world gives. Do not let your hearts be troubled, do not let it be fearful." John 14:27

Jesus is saying to us that His peace is different from the world's peace. He was letting his disciples in on a very important principle that despite the troubling situation about to occur, they did not need to be troubled or afraid because his peace was greater than anything they had ever known. This chapter explains the importance of having a relationship of peace: BEHOLD, I WILL BRING IT HEALTH AND HEALING; AND I WILL HEAL YOU AND WILL REVEAL UNTO YOU THE ABUNDANCE OF PEACE AND TRUTH. (JEREMIAH 33:6)

I love this scripture Numbers 6:24-26: "The Lord bless you and keep you; The Lord makes his face shine upon you and be gracious to you; The Lord lifts up His countenance upon you and give you peace." Finally, through trials or testing, whatever you ask in my name and I will do it, so that the Father may be glorified."

Chapter Four:
"FAITH OF THE FATHER'S LOVE"

On April 6, 2016, as I was waking up, I had no breakfast. I was NPO because I was getting ready to go to surgery at 10:00 AM. When I got ready, the first thing I did was I got on my knees and started praying with my husband in my bedroom and asking God to increase my faith through the process while going to surgery. Then, I was walking to the living room to talk with my lovely Daddy and sat down on his lap. I told my Daddy that I was going to have surgery this morning, but I am coming back and then my Daddy started praying for me and gave me a big hug and kiss. He said, I will be right here waiting for you sitting down on my couch when you come back. My Daddy had so much faith that everything was gonna be alright. He said, (Mijia) "Daughter, because we have already prayed, and asked God to heal you, and to be with the doctors and nurses, so have faith and believe, expect positive results." My daddy loves to meditate on this scripture in the book of *Mark 9:23 Jesus said to him, "if you can believe, all things are possible to him who believes."* My Daddy did not know how much pain I was feeling or the true nature of my condition. I felt my Daddy knew that our Heavenly Father would be by my side through the whole surgery. Every day I would meditate on this scripture: *Psalm 118:17 "I will not die, but I will live and proclaim what the Lord has done."* That was my favorite scripture I repeated to myself over and over. My prayer was "Jesus, you know, I have four beautiful children, also my husband and my dad to take care of. I am asking you by faith to give me a second chance to enjoy seeing my children grow up, my children to graduate from high school and to attend college; also, to see them married; to see my grandchildren." As the Doctors were getting ready to prepare the operating room, my family and I got into a circle and prayed with my close friends Michael and Janie Hernandez to believe for a miracle and that the surgery would be successful. I had to encourage my family, "I'm coming back. I'm not going to take too long in the surgery." I just want you to remember that I will always love you; I will see you all in a little bit!"

I gave them a big kiss and hugs. Through this journey, I had to stay focused in a positive way and to activate my faith. Thank you, Lord for giving me your covenant of peace to guard my heart and my mind also for my family. "The Lord is my Shepherd; I have all that I need. He leads the beside peaceful streams he renews my strength." The hardest thing was for me to leave my family in the waiting room for a long time. I said to my family, "Let me open my prayer book before going to surgery." God gave me this scripture, Jesus said to me, in the book of *Mark 5:34* ***"Daughter, your faith has made you well; go in peace and be healed of your affliction." Mark 5:34.***

When the doctors were getting me ready to take me to the operating room, I had to believe and have faith, to be strong and to know that God is by my side close to my bed in the operating room and he will not move from my side. Jesus, turn your face towards me and give me peace. O' Mighty God, I thank you that you are my creator who knows exactly what is wrong with my body; hear my prayer, I am asking you to give wisdom and direction to the surgeon, doctors, and the nurse to know exactly what needs to be done to restore the inside of my colon, that my operation would be successful with no complications. Holy Spirit, I pray for a fresh anointing on the doctors and nurses and on their hands and clarity in their minds in the operating room. Heavenly Father, I thank you that you're my defender, and that you give victory in my life. You are in control. Bring health and healing to me because you love me. I even asked the surgeon and doctor if we could pray for the surgery to be a success and she said 'Yes', go ahead. She said to me; you start the prayer, and I will end the prayer. At the time of the surgery, the lower part of my colon was identified to be very attached and ingrained in the bladder, probably due to the previous inflammatory process. Surgery was very difficult to identify the bladder itself, so the bladder was opened, and the inside of the bladder explored and identified as ureteral orifices in the normal location, effluxion; clear urine and the foley catheter in place. The surgery was about six hours because it was very critical. I had a large tumor on my colon the size of iceberg lettuce. When the surgery was complete and I was taken to the ICU, my daughter Magaly decided to stay the night and to take care of me. She never fell asleep and stayed awake and meditated on the word of God and she worshiped and prayed to God that he would heal me. When, I was in the hospital bed, I heard the Holy Spirit say for us to remember he will always be with us in the middle of the storm. He alone is the anchor of our soul, and His Love surrounds us. Daily I had to exercise and confess my faith and commitment to the love of God when I chose to obey His word. When we have an active faith, we can receive supernatural healing, deliverance, provision, and protection.

On Friday morning, the colonoscopy doctor came to the room to visit my husband and I, to give us the outcome of the surgery and he said that it is cancer in your colon. I told the doctor, "I do not think so, because I did not hear that from God. He is Alpha and Omega; God knows from the beginning to the end of my life." The doctor said, "Mrs. Escalera do you have any questions?" I said, "No I will wait for the Surgeon to finalize my results." When the colonoscopy doctor said that to me, my husband started crying. I am sorry, "But, Honey why are you crying? Whose report are we going to believe the doctors or God's report?" I stood in authority, I said, "NO, I DON'T HAVE CANCER." I said, to my husband, "Why are we going to open the door to the enemy lies. When we have not heard from the surgeon, and she was the one who laid hands on me during the surgery." Let's wait and see what the surgeon says. Let's pray for peace.

On Friday evening the surgeon came to the room, and I asked her, "I want to know how the surgery went because the colonoscopy doctor said that it was cancer. But I wanted to hear from you, could you read your Leap Notes and tell me what you found in my colon?" And she said, "Mrs. Escalera are you ready to hear the great news?" I said, "Yes, I am ready." You don't have Cancer it is **Negative**. Starting from today on, you can eat whatever you want, you are healed and clean." I said, Thank you Jesus! My husband I were crying tears of joy. I was very excited for the great news. I could eat again. I missed out on so much of eating chicken tacos with avocado, all good food. The Lord has given us the gift of faith for this purpose. The more we hear about the gifts of God, the more faith you will receive to draw closer to God. The Lord desires that we use our faith to put a deposit on our gifts from God.

Through my faith, I put a demand on the anointing of God to be present in the surgery room for the doctors and nurses. I allowed the faith seed of the word of God concerning my healing to be planted in me. God has successfully reaped the healing harvest for my life and yours as well. I had to believe in healing, without the healing seed from God's word planted in my heart, I had nothing in the ground to produce the harvest. I had to base it on the real faith that God has restored my health. Several times since, I have learned to walk in faith. I continually feed myself with God's word in order to keep the word producing the force of faith. Here are some declarations and scriptures I received in faith for healing, and that I use on a daily basis, and you can use throughout your journey:

-I live by faith. I walk by faith and not by sight. (2 Cor.5:7)

-Have faith in God. (Mark 11:22)

-Because you know that the testing of your faith produces perseverance. (James 1:3)

-Let us hold fast the confession of our hope without wavering; for He who promised is faithful. (Hebrews 10:23)

-For by grace you have been saved through Faith. (Ephesians 2:8)

-That your faith should not be in the wisdom of men but in the power of God (1Corinthians 2:5)

-But without faith it is impossible to please God; for he that comes to God must believe that He is, and that He is a rewarder of those who diligently seek him. (Hebrews 11:6)

-But let him ask in faith, with no doubting, for he who doubts is like a wave of the sea driven and tossed by wind. (James 1:6)

-Receive one who is weak in the faith, but not to disputes over doubtful things. (Romans 14:1)

-So, faith comes from hearing, and hearing through the word of God. (Romans 10:17)

-Increase my faith our ability to confidently trust in God and in His power. (Luke 17:5)

-And all these, having obtained a good testimony through faith (Hebrews 11:39-40)

-I decree and declare that by faith I will walk through my trials on dry ground, and my enemies will be drowned. (Heb.11:29)

-Now faith is the substance of things hoped for, the evidence of things not seen. (Heb. 11:1)

-But Jesus turned around, and when He saw her He said, "Be of good cheer, daughter; your faith has made you well" (Matthew 9:22)

-Now this is the confidence that we have in Him, that if we ask anything according to His will, He hears us. (1 John 5:14)

Dear Father, I am thankful surely your goodness and your mercy never fails me all my days, He has been faithful to me. He has been so good; with every breath that I am able to take; I will praise you for the goodness of your love. I thank you God, I'm going to see your victory for the battle belongs to you Lord; He takes what the enemy meant for evil, and He will turn it for good. I thank you for your truth, *"no weapon that is formed against you will prosper," Isaiah 54:17* We are secure in God's hands, and He tells us to "stand firm." Whether in life, or in death, we may always be still and know to recognize that God is our refuge.

Chapter Five:
"FORGIVE OTHERS"

I had to build myself up and encourage myself through prayer most of the time. I asked God to forgive me from any sin that I carried in my heart; to empty out any envy or strife against anyone, to release any unforgiveness, to be delivered from all sickness that I was feeling inside of me. It started with my siblings. If I caused any harm in any way and also with my children and husband; also, my daddy and my mom, I wanted to be forgiven. I wanted to move forward to experience the spirit of joy in my life, it was MANDATORY for me to forgive all those who hurt me and also the hurt I caused them too. So, I could move on with my life and leave the pain, past and hurt all behind. There's no other way I could keep going and to come to a place of inner peace and self-love until I did this. Forgiveness sets us free. You have to understand that. You have to want this freedom more than the pain you are holding onto. Too often we beat ourselves up over things that happened in the past. We do the best we can with what we know and how we feel. You are not to blame for anything that happened. You need to stop beating yourself up, take a moment to forgive yourself and let it go. What's done is done and there's nothing you can do differently now except to learn and grow from what happened. Forgiving others doesn't mean we condone their behavior. Nope, not at all. When we forgive the people who hurt us, we are releasing them from our minds and our hearts and moving on without the built up and stored anger, hatred, hurt, excruciating pain and grudges. They don't even have to know you forgave them! You don't do it for them, you do it for you, and I had to do it for myself. It frees up your power, heals your body, and your soul, mind and spirit.

When we withhold our forgiveness, in other words when holding onto a grudge, it negatively affects every part of our lives. On a physical level, when we choose not to forget, it allows bitterness and resentment to take over which increases stress. Which in turn can lead to high blood pressure, heart disease, diabetes and many other illnesses. God does that over and over again in our lifetime, no sin is too big that it cannot be thrown into

God's Ocean of forgiveness. Luke 11:4, "And forgive us our sins; for we also forgive every one that is indebted to us. And lead us not into temptation; but deliver us from evil." I needed to forgive others. I even called people I thought I might have offended after I became sick because I had been so irritable. I want to share with you how God can take your sin, forgive that sin and then set you free from all of your burdens and bondage and also sickness. Forgiveness can help bring healing and help us to feel better physically, but it can also help us emotionally. Forgive them to the point where you actually feel yourself cleansed of resentment and bitterness and are actually praying for them. Forgiveness opens up a pathway to a new place of peace where you can persist in your life. When you forgive, it will heal you and allow you to move on in life with meaning and purpose. Forgiveness is strong medicine. I'm thankful to God because He gives us his grace and his mercy to forgive others. It had a huge effect on me, and it could break down my ability to connect with God. "Lord, teach us to pray just as you also taught the disciples. He said to them, *Our Father in heaven, hallowed be your name. Your kingdom come. Your will be done on earth as it is in heaven. Give us each day our daily bread. And forgive us our sins, for we also forgive everyone who is indebted to us. And do not lead us into temptation but deliver us from the evil one." Luke 11:1-4.* For if you forgive men when they sin against you, your heavenly Father will also forgive you. But if you do not forgive men their sins, your Father will not forgive your sins. I SEE BENEATH THE SURFACE OF UNFORGIVENESS. Why should I forgive? Christ commands it "... forgive as..." Keep on forgiving others then. Ask God for wisdom to show you how to help others live the life that God meant for them to live, how to be set free from unforgiveness. If you have to do it Seventy Times Seventy, then do so with happiness. God never stops forgiving you, why should we ever stop forgiving others? It is forgiveness that breaks this cycle. However, it is unforgiveness that messes up the mind and keeps us full of anger and forgiveness shows that there is another way to live. When you forgive one another, you keep your own mind full of peace, your own heart full of love, and your own soul full of joy. You pass these precious gifts along to them as well. You live the way that God meant for you to live, and you show everyone around you how a child of God can make this world a better and more loving place. "Therefore, if you bring your gift to the altar and there remember that your brother has something against you, leave your gift there in front of the altar, and go your way. First be reconciled to your brother; and then come and offer your gift." Matthew 5:23-24. "So My heavenly Father also will do to you, if each of you from his Heart, do not forgive his brother their trespasses." Matthew 18:35 I heard the Holy Spirit say, "How can you say you love me when you cannot forgive those who hurt you?" Forgiveness frees us and cleanses our heart of strife, selfishness and discontent. When we become aware of the presence of the Lord in our heart, we no longer want to hold onto ungodly attitudes. God subdues the power of sin in us and works to change us as we set our minds on and seek after the things that gratify the Holy Spirit. When we feel defeated and condemned by every mistake we make, it weakens us. Instead of using our spiritual energy to feel bad about ourselves, we should use it to press on to new levels in God. Any believer who has a right heart attitude towards God will continually press toward perfection, but none of us will totally arrive at perfection as long as we are flesh and bones and, in a body, living in the present world. God, in His grace and mercy, has made provision for our sins, faults, weaknesses, infirmities, and failures. That provision is forgiveness.

When you fail, receive God's forgiveness, but don't stop trying to do better. Here are some of my favorite scriptures I stand on daily they help me to gain strength: "Forgive the transgression of your brothers and their sin, for they did you wrong." (Gen 50:17)

"Forgive my sin only this once [more], and pray and entreat the Lord your God, so that He will remove this [plague of] death from me." (Exodus 10:17)

"Forgive your people who have sinned against you and all the transgressions which they have committed against you." (1Kings 8:50)

 "Hear in heaven, your dwelling place; hear and forgive." (1Kings

8:30)

"Then hear in heaven your dwelling place and forgive my sin and

give to each according to my ways, you alone know my heart." (1 Kings 8:39)

"Then hear thou in heaven thy dwelling place, and forgive, and do, and give to every man according to his ways, whose heart thou knowest; (for thou, even though only, knowest the hearts of all the children of men;)" (1 Kings 8:39)

"Then hear thou in heaven, and forgive the sin of thy people Israel, and bring them again unto the land which thou gavest unto their fathers." (1 Kings 8:34)

"And my people, who are called by my name, humble themselves, and pray and seek (crave, require as a necessity) My face and turn from their wicked ways, then I will hear [them] from heaven, and forgive their sin and heal their land." (2 Chron. 7:14)

"Look upon my affliction and my trouble and forgive all my sins." (Psalms 25:18)

"For you, O Lord, are good, and ready to forgive [my sins, sending them away, completely letting them go forever and ever] and abundant in lovingkindness and overflowing in mercy to all those who call upon You." (Psalms 86:5)

This story is a great example of when Jesus confronts a crowd about to stone a woman who was caught in the crime of adultery. Jesus said to the crowd, "Let anyone among you who is without sin be the first to throw a stone at her." (John 8:7) And no one moves to attack the woman, Jesus is so merciful to let her go and not even condemn the woman. Go your way, and from now on do not sin again. (John 8:11)

When we repent and ask God to forgive us of every sin we have ever committed, whether large or small, we can be thankful to Jesus for forgiving us. I recognize that many times I have sinned against others and how I seek forgiveness. "Jesus, I know you are so merciful to forgive me, but I also ask that you help me with my emotions and sustain me and heal me from all my pain and the shame that I am experiencing. Jesus, I love you so much because you still care for me. I am a child of God and give me the power to make it through this season. Amen."

Chapter Six:
"OVERCOME BY THE BLOOD OF THE LAMB"

Because of the power of the blood of Jesus, you and I can come boldly into His presence. *"In Him we have redemption through His Blood, the forgiveness of sins, according to the riches of His grace." Ephesians 1:7* When I applied the blood of Jesus, I knew I would receive my healing. I constantly need to remind myself that the blood gives me strength from day to day, it will never lose its power.

On April 6, 2016, I received the fullness and freedom of His healing power through his Blood during a time of surgery. I didn't want to miss the opportunity when the doctors told me, Mrs. Escalera, you will need a blood transfusion because you are 7% percent anemic and need 3 pints of blood. I took the opportunity to depend on the Blood of Jesus. I began to pray Thank you, "Jesus, you know that I'm going through this, but I'm asking you, in faith for you to stay beside my bed when the doctors and nurses are operating on me; please do not move from my side. Thank you, Jesus, for the blood you shed for me at the cross, that I know the Blood of Jesus will wash me clean whiter than snow. Your Blood will refine me again my whole body, it will give me a brand new colon, In Jesus' Name. I believe, in Your Blood, it is the measure of my faith, more than I deserve. Thank you, Jesus, you are still sitting on the throne to watch over me and thank you for those who donated the blood and for those who also need blood transfusions. He consecrated himself for us through the blood of Jesus he purchased salvation for us. When I finished praying, I fell in a deep sleep, and I didn't know what happened next. I didn't hear the doctors and nurses talking in the operation room.

The surgery lasted from 10am until 4pm when I was taken to ICU. I was not feeling pain, and I did not know that I had 100 staples in my stomach, and two days after the surgery, I was fragile and trying to walk. But I know Jesus' sacrifice covered every area of man's existence. Jesus bore spiritual torment, torture, mental distress, worry, and fear as well as physical pain and sickness and all disease.

But according to *Isaiah 53:4-5 "But He was wounded for our transgressions and bruised for our iniquities; The chastisement for our peace was upon Him, and by His stripes we are healed."*

Every day I will say, Thank you God. I am delivered from sin and sickness. I had to encourage myself to exercise the authority God has given me by pleading the blood of Jesus. I refused to listen to any lies from the devil and every evil word that was spoken over me. When I received the revelation that the blood of Jesus has provided redemption, fellowship, healing, protection, and authority over the devil's lies, Jesus gave His life and shed His blood to reconcile us from sin and sickness if we believe in Him. According to *1 John 1:7 "But if we walk in the light, as he is the light, we have fellowship with one another, and the blood of Jesus cleanses us from all sin."* The power of the blood of Jesus is enough to overcome everything coming against our health. This is how to live a life of God's victory and to know, it's the life for us that Jesus died for. I would always read my bible when I was in hospital to encourage myself. Jesus gave me this scripture *Revelation 12:11, "And they overcame by the Blood of the Lamb, and by the word of their testimony."* I had to allow the fullness of the power of the blood to operate in my life. Every night while going to bed, I turned on YouTube and listened to this song:

> *"Nothing but the Blood of Jesus"*
> *What can wash away my sin?*
> *Nothing but the blood of Jesus*
> *What can make me whole again?*
> *Nothing but the blood of Jesus*
> *Oh! Precious is the flow*
> *That makes me white as snow*
> *No other fount I know*
> *Nothing but the blood of Jesus."*

But the woman with the issue of blood believed. She believed enough to press through the crowds, reach out, and touch the healer herself. In Luke 8:46, Jesus says, "Somebody touched me, for I perceived power going out from me." The woman drew healing power out of Him with her faith. I had faith that I would be healed, and I drew out the healing power of God. His power is released on my behalf. This woman heard of Jesus. She had heard about the healing anointing that was upon Him. She heard that a prophet of God was ministering in Israel. God is love and the greatest expression of His love towards us is the blood of Jesus. That love covers every need man has had, or ever will have. And every time we apply the blood, we experience an outpouring of this love. It is love, through the blood, that has created a barrier between you and all the works of the devil. I had to elevate the blood of Jesus to the same place in my heart that it has in God's heart and awaken in my spirit those powerful things the blood has procured for me. The power of the blood of Jesus has provided everything I need to live a life of victory, including redemption, fellowship, healing, protection and authority over the devil. The greatest thing the blood of Jesus accomplished was this, "It washed all my sins away and made me clean and pure and white as snow." From the minute I prayed during the surgery, I received the power of His blood in me. Every day I had the right to exercise that authority by pleading what the blood of Jesus has done for me and refuse to give the enemy even one small inch of territory. Satan is a defeated foe, and through the precious blood of Jesus, I'm victorious! One way I recognized that the blood provided fellowship with God is through the taking of communion every morning and believing in faith that I'm Healed. Jesus said, "Do this in remembrance of me, for every time you eat this bread and drink this cup, you are representing and signifying and proclaiming, the face of the Lord's death until he comes {again}." 1 Corinthians 11:23- 26. I personally believe that communion is another way that we express outwardly what is happening inwardly. The Bible says that every time we eat the bread and drink the cup, we are remembering Christ' body and His blood and proclaiming His death until He comes back. As I was watching Pastor Joseph Prince, in March 2016, he was teaching "The Power of The Holy Communion." Pastor Joseph Prince said, "by his stripes your cancer died, by his stripes high blood pressure is normalized in Jesus' Name." Mark 14:22, "And as they were eating, Jesus took bread, blessed and broke it, and gave it to them and said, "Take, eat, this My body.' 23) Then He took the cup, and when He had given thanks He gave it to them, and they all drank from it. 24) And he said to them, "This is My blood of the new covenant, which is shed for many 25) Assuredly, I say to you, I will no longer drink of the fruit of the vine until that day when I drink it new in the kingdom of God."

We need to understand that when we take Communion, we are making a declaration of faith with our actions and not just with what we say we believe in our hearts. That's why Communion bridges a deeper relationship and fellowship with God. Observance—it's recognition of (and fellowship with) what God did for us through the blood of Jesus. You are a friend of God, John 15:15. When I take communion in the mornings, I always say, "Lord Jesus as I take this bread, I am taking You as my Living Bread. As long as I eat of You and fellowship with You, I will be satisfied. As I take this drink, I am drinking Living Water. As long as I drink of You and fellowship with You, I will be satisfied to the point where I am not disturbed; no matter what my outward circumstances may be. I am declaring by the taking of this Communion, Lord Jesus, that you are all I need in life to be truly content and fulfilled." The Lord gave me this song early in the morning:

> *"Blessed assurance, Jesus is mine*
> *O what a foretaste of glory divine*
> *Heir of salvation, purchased of God*
> *Born of His Spirit, washed in His blood*
> *Perfect submission, all is at rest*

I in my Savior am happy and blessed

Watching and waiting, looking above

Filled with His goodness, lost in His love

This is my story, this is my song

Praising my Savior all the day long

This is my story, this is my song

Praising my Savior all day long."

The Blood of Jesus is most powerful; it is absolutely the most precious gift God has offered us. "In Him we have redemption through His blood, the forgiveness of sins, according to the riches of His grace." Ephesians 1:7

Chapter Seven: "IT'S FINISHED AT THE CROSS"

On May 6, 2016, at 7:38 AM on a Friday morning, I was praying with my son Elijah. He was eleven years old, in my master bedroom. I was praying asking God for a BIG present for Mother's Day and to perform a sign and to reveal that I am healed. Elijah said, "Mom, mom you want to see this!" I said, "Elijah please do not interrupt." He said, "But mom lookup, it's a sign of the cross." I told Elijah, "What! Oh God, you really answered our prayers. Let's take a picture because Jesus wants us to expose the cross around the world." The cross appeared through the reflection of the blinds through the windows in my master bedroom. I was weeping, and I could not stop crying because Jesus really showed up that Friday morning. He revealed to my son the symbol of the cross. It is a true blessing for Elijah (my son) to know that Jesus sacrificed his body at the "Cross." It truly blessed my soul to know, "The Cross Has the Final Word." Hebrews 12:2 "Looking unto to Jesus the author and finisher of our faith; who for the joy that was set before him endured the cross, despising the shame, and is set down at the right hand of the throne of God." This chapter will teach you how God worked miracles through his son Jesus: Acts 2:22 "Men of Israel, listen to these words: Jesus of Nazareth, a man attested to you by God with miracles and wonders and signs which God performed through Him in your midst, just as you yourselves know." The book of 2 Kings 20:8-11, Hezekiah asked Isaiah, "What will be the sign that the Lord will heal me and that I will go up to the temple of the Lord on the third day from now?" Isaiah answered, "This is the Lord's sign to you that the Lord will do what he has promised: Shall the shadow go forward. While Prophet Isaiah extended his hand to heal..." We know the story in the sixth month the angel was sent from God unto a city of Galilee, to the town of Nazareth. The angel came in unto Mary to bring her great news; Mary is highly favored with God. But the angel said unto Mary, "Fear Not, Mary behold thou shalt conceive and give birth to a son you shall call his name Jesus. He shall be great and will be called the son of the Highest: The Lord God will give him the throne of his father David. Mary was astonished and Mary said to the angel, how shall this be, seeing I know not a man? The angel answered and said unto her, The Holy Spirit will come upon you, and the power of the Highest will overshadow you." Luke 1:35 Mary was a willing servant who trusted God and showed obedience and submission to His calling. Her mission was to witness the glory of the Son of God, to see his first miracles. Jesus performed his first miracle at the wedding in Cana of Galilee; and the mother of Jesus was there. When the wine ran out, the mother of Jesus said unto him, "They have no wine." Mary believed in Jesus that he could turn the water to wine. But Jesus told her mother, "Woman, what should I do with thee? Mine hour has not yet come." And there was a certain nobleman whose son was sick in Capernaum. When he heard that Jesus had come out of Judea into Galilee, he went to Him and implored Him to come down and heal his son, for he was at the point of death. Then Jesus said to him, "Unless you people see signs and wonders, you will by no means believe." The nobleman said to Him, "Sir, come down before my child dies!" Jesus said to him, "Go your way; your son lives."

So, the man believed the word that Jesus spoke to him, and he went his way. Jesus performed many miracles on earth; and his disciples believed in him.

This is a powerful excerpt from the bible about how Judas betrays Jesus, because of the betrayal it would allow God's plan to come to pass. Matthew 26 "Now on the first day of the feast of Unleavened Bread the disciples came to Jesus and asked, "Where do you want us to prepare the Passover so you may eat it 18) My time is near; I am celebrating the Passover at your place with my disciples. So, the disciples did as Jesus had directed them and prepared the Passover. When evening had come, He sat down with the Twelve. Now as they were eating, He said, "Assuredly, I say to you, one of you will betray me." He answered and said, "He who dipped his hand with me in the dish will betray me." Then Judas, who was betraying Him, answered and said, "Rabbi, is it I?" He said to him, "You have said it." Judas leaves the supper he that betrayed him gave them a sigh, saying, "Whomsoever I shall kiss, that same is he: hold him fast." Judas goes with a great multitude with swords and staves, the chief priests and elders of the people took counsel against Jesus to put him to death, on that morning. Then the soldiers of the governor took Jesus into the common hall and gathered unto him the whole band of soldiers. And they stripped him and put on him a scarlet robe. And when they had planted a crown of thorns, they put it upon his head, and a reed in high hand: and they bowed the knee before him and mocked and spit upon Jesus saying, "Hail, King of the Jews!" And after that they had mocked him, they took the robe off from him and put his own raiment on him and led him away to crucify him." John 19:34 "But one of the soldiers pierced his side with a spear, and immediately blood and water came out. And he who has seen has testified, and testimony is true; and he knows that he is telling the truth, so that you may believe. "They shall look on Him whom they pierced." Matthew 27:50 "And When Jesus had cried out again in a loud voice, he gave up his spirit from His body in submission to His Father's plan." Matthew 28:1 "And, behold, there was a great earthquake: for the angel of the Lord descended from heaven, and came and rolled back the stone from the door, and sat upon it. And the angel answered and said unto the women, "Do not be afraid; for I know that you are looking for Jesus who has been crucified. He is not here, for He is risen, Just as He said. Come! See the place where He was lying. Then go quickly and tell His disciples that He has risen from the dead; and behold, He is going ahead of you into Galilee as Jesus promised. There you will see Him. So the women left the tomb quickly with fear and great joy, and ran to tell the good news to the disciples. And as they went, suddenly, Jesus met them, saying, "REJOICE!" And they went to Him and took hold of His feet and worshiped Him. But if the Spirit of him that raised up Jesus from the dead dwell in you, he that raised up Christ from the dead shall also quicken your mortal bodies by his Spirit that dwells in you." I recall a time when my eyes were closed, and my son Elijah did not want me to lose sight of this God given opportunity for a deep experience of the Cross of Jesus. Thank you, Jesus for answering my prayer. It was so beautiful that I did not want it to go away from my wall. As tears rolled down my cheeks, I could feel the presence of the Lord fill my soul. I was just praising God for my miracle. How we are so blessed that Jesus took on our sins at the cross to redeem us, he makes us new by His resurrection to give us a brand-new life. When we see the cross, we have freedom and liberty from sin and all sickness. Jesus used the occasion to show us in the book of Matthew 16:24, "Then said Jesus unto his disciples, if any man will come after me, let him deny himself and take up his cross, and follow me." I have entered into a new purpose of my life to enjoy the journey, to draw closer to God; to stay committed to his promise. Galatians 2:20, "I am crucified with Christ: nevertheless I live; yet not I, but Christ liveth in me: and the life which I now live in the flesh I live by the faith of the Son of God, who loved me, and gave himself for us." Jesus died on the cross, God gave the life of His Son to set us free from the bondage of sickness. To receive healing is without a doubt a part of our redemption that was purchased for your freedom from sickness as well as sin, once for all. During my time of worship, I would listen to my favorite song 1) Grace to Grace 2) Miracles 3) At the Cross. 4) Jesus, I Believe in You. I belong to you. The reason that I live is because I can enter into holiness and a place of worship having an authentic relationship with God, through the Messiah. This is how God wants us to enter into the spirit of believing, knowing that God can manifest miracles to heal all your pain. John 3:36, "He who believes and trusts in the Son and accepts Him has everlasting life: but he who believeth not the Son shall not see life."

It is written in Romans 10:13, "For whoever calls on the name of the Lord in prayer will be saved." Jesus Christ paid the price for our sin so that we don't have to. According to the book of 1 Corinthians 15:4, "The truth is that Christ died on the cross, was buried, he was raised on the third day and is alive today, Jesus is now seated at the right hand of the Father, where He will remain until He returns, a time which only God Knows." You could certainly apply this to learning and gaining new knowledge. "You will know the truth, and the truth will set me and you free." John 8:32. It's time for us to receive the freedom to be free from all the sin bondage and transgression of the past, present and future. When it perceives the truth, there comes to it a power. The inheritance is 1 Peter 1:3, "Blessed be the God and Father of our Lord Jesus Christ, who according to His abundant mercy has begotten us again to a living hope through the resurrection of Jesus Christ from the dead." "For I know that my Redeemer lives and at the last he will stand upon the earth." Job 19:25 "Jesus you make all things new." You have won the victory and all power is yours, your glory: Jesus overcame he is our Conqueror. He gives us victories, our Redeemer. He is our closest and best friend.

Let your light shine upon us, so others, can see your glory and purpose. He will reflect your peace and hope for a world that so desperately needs your presence and healing and deliverance. John 19:30, "When Jesus therefore had received the vinegar, he said, "IT IS FINISHED:" and he bowed his head and gave up His spirit."

Reference Scriptures:

Jeremiah 31:3; Zephaniah 3:17; John 15:12-16; 1 John 4:9-10 Isaiah 41:10: Matthew 1:23; John 14:16-18; Revelation 3:4-6 2 Samuel 22:31; 2 Cor 1:20-22; Hebrews 6:18; 2 Peter 1:3-4 Psalm 30:10-12; Matthew 11:28-30; 2 Cor 1:5; 1 Peter 5:10 Psalm 49:15; Job 23:10; Galatians 4:4-6; Hebrews 9:11-5 Psalm 14:15-19; Matthew 6:33; Phil 4:19; 2 Cor 9:8-10 Isaiah 55:7; Romans 4:24 Hebrews 10:10; 1 John 1:9 Deut. 31:6; Psalm 55:22; John 16:33; Ephesians 3:16 Jeremiah 33:3; Psalm 30:2-3; Hosea 6:3; Luke 11:10-13 Psalm 37:5; Proverbs 2:8; Isaiah 30:21; John 16:13 Psalm 6:9; Psalm 28:6-7: Matthew 7:7 1 John 5:14-15